One-Minute BEDTIME DEVOTIONS

Marie D. Jones

Publications International, Ltd.

Marie D. Jones is an ordained minister and a contributing author to numerous books, including *Sisters, Mother, Grandmother, Friends, Graduation, Wedding,* and *A Mother's Daily Prayer Book.* She is a widely published writer and can be reached through her Web site, www.mariedjones.com.

Additional quotations provided by: Elaine Write Colvin, Elaine Creasman, Ellen F. Pill, and Donna Shryer.

All Scripture quotations are taken from the *New Revised Standard Version* of the Bible. Copyright © 1989 by the Division of Christian Education of the National Council of the Churches of Christ in the USA. Used by permission. All rights reserved.

Cover photos: Brand X Pictures; Getty Images

Louis Weber, CEO
Publications International, Ltd.
7373 North Cicero Avenue
Lincolnwood, Illinois 60712

ISBN-13: 978-1-4127-0428-1
ISBN-10: 1-4127-0428-6

Manufactured in U.S.A.

8 7 6 5 4 3 2 1

CONTENTS

IT ONLY TAKES A MINUTE ...

~~~

*E*ven just a moment spent in devotional prayer can lead to a lifetime filled with blessings. Praising God, telling him how your day went, and asking for his help and wisdom is what connects you to his loving and infinite presence, just as time spent thinking about God's will and word serves to comfort and heal you. Talking to God can be part of your daily routine; after all, your message to God doesn't have to be long and wordy.

The prayers, thoughts, and Bible verses in *One-Minute Bedtime Devotions* are intended to help you end each day with a special moment of grace. By taking a minute or two each evening to turn inward, you'll find that God is, and always has been, waiting to help you. He wants what is best for you and, in his omniscience, knows how you may best accomplish that. Whether you are singing his praises, asking for spiritual healing, or seeking a deeper understanding of his will, God not only listens, but he also responds with wisdom, comfort, and guidance.

Spend a devotional moment this evening with *One-Minute Bedtime Devotions.* Make this book part of your bedtime preparations. As time goes on, you may notice that blessings and miracles "suddenly" appear—though often they were there all the time, waiting for you to take notice. In the quiet solitude of devotion, you are given the chance to be heard by a power far greater than yourself, a power that can lift you up when you are lonely, lost, and afraid; a power that further blesses a grateful heart and fulfills a joyful spirit.

It only takes a minute to talk to God. The result is an eternity of knowing you are loved and cared for in return.

Rejoice always, pray without ceasing, give thanks in all circumstances; for this is the will of God in Christ Jesus for you.
—1 Thessalonians 5:16–18

Remembering Our Blessings

BLESSINGS OF SUCCESS

I pray tonight for the blessing of a peaceful rest. I've worked hard toward my goals, and it is time to be grateful for the positive rewards I've experienced as a result of my work. But let me never forget to be grateful to you, God, for making all the good things in my life possible. Because of my faith in you and the knowledge that you will always guide me in the direction of your will, I see amazing miracles and blessings occur each and every day. For that I thank you.

If one advances confidently in the direction of his dreams, and endeavors to live the life he has imagined, he will meet with a success unexpected in common hours.

—Henry David Thoreau

GOD'S GIFTS

Blessed be the Lord, who daily bears us up;
God is our salvation.
—Psalm 68:19

God, help me to see the blessings right in front
of me, because sometimes life has a way
of clouding my vision until all I can see is the black cloud
of my problems. I often forget at the end of each day
that I have indeed been given many wonderful lessons and
blessings to help me grow as a person and become stronger
and more serene. By changing my focus back to your abiding
love, I know the cloud will dissipate and the goodness of
my life will once again become clear to me. I pray my focus
will stay on the gifts and not on the problems.

BLESSED SOLITUDE

*M*ay you recognize today that being alone is not always being lonely, nor that solitude always means you must have a problem to solve. With everyone far away, rejoice in the blessing of your quietness.

Of all good gifts that the Lord lets fall,
Is not silence the best of all?
The deep, sweet hush when the song is closed,
And every sound but a voiceless ghost;
And every sigh, as we listening leant,
A breathless quiet of vast content?
The laughs we laughed have a purer ring
With but their memory echoing;
So of all good gifts that the Lord lets fall,
Is not silence the best of all?
—James Whitcomb Riley, "Best of All"

Amazement

***In his hand is the life of every living thing and the
breath of every human being.***
—Job 12:10

God of all creation, I never cease to be amazed by
the work of your hands. Today, when I
looked outside and saw the glories of the day
beginning to emerge, I was reminded of all the ways you
are working to restore me and bring me into the light.
Thank you, Lord, for caring enough about me to
consistently renew me and give me hope that each day
I live is a day worth celebrating. I'm glad my life is in
your hands.

The beauty of creation inspires me to live a life where I, too,
can create something beautiful.

Sunrise, Sunset

Praise him, sun and moon.
Let them praise the name of the Lord,
for he commanded and they were created.
—Psalm 148:3, 5

Creator God, I especially want to thank you for two spectacular times of day: sunrise and sunset. When I'm present at one of these events, I'm drawn into silence, and yet my heart beats faster with the wonder and glory of what I see. The light that spreads across the earth and illumines the sky causes me to long for the light of your presence. Be always near me, dear Lord.

Every sunset which I witness inspires me with
the desire to go to a West as distant and as fair
as that into which the sun goes down.
—Henry David Thoreau, "Walking"

THE BLESSINGS OF THIS DAY

*G*od, you have seen fit to bless me with so many
wonderful things. My life has been filled with
happiness and sadness, and I've learned and grown
so much from both. As I wind down for the night,
I cannot help but think about the blessings that even this
one day has brought me. Thank you for the small events
of the day, the little things that make me stop and smile and
know that all is right in heaven, just as it is here on Earth.

Happy is the man, and happy he alone,
He, who can call today his own;
He, who secure within, can say,
Tomorrow do their worst, for I have lived today.
—John Dryden

A LIGHT IN THE WORLD

For the Lord God is a sun and shield;
he bestows favor and honor.
No good thing does the Lord withhold from
those who walk uprightly.
—Psalm 84:11

I pray tonight not just for blessings, Lord, but also to be a blessing to others. When all I do is take and receive, I find I am not truly happy. But when I am giving my service and time to others, or even just giving someone a smile, I feel as though I matter and make a difference. Help me to see not only the blessings I have, but also what a blessing I can be in a world that truly needs more light and love.

LEAVING A MARK

*B*less our work, Lord of vineyards and seas.
We long to leave a mark as visible as a building or a bridge.
We yearn to be connected with what we do and
to do something that matters.

Show us that what we do is as indelible as a handprint on
fresh concrete, even though our mark may be in spots no one
else can see right now. Harvest comes in its own sweet time.

Bless our left-behind marks, for with you as our
foundation, our work is as essential to the overall
structure of life as a concrete pillar.

How good to get this promotion!
And how I've waited for this day! Now that it is here,
I thank you for the chance to savor it. A job well done is
a good thing, I know. I will celebrate before your smiling eyes
and give you credit, too. Because, after all, everything
I am and have comes from your gracious hand.

MY MIRACLES

Then afterward, I will pour out my spirit on all flesh;
your sons and your daughters shall prophesy,
your old men shall dream dreams...
—Joel 2:28

ord, I don't want to ask for anything tonight.
Instead, I want to thank you for all my miracles. Thank you
for my family and all the joy and laughter and even the tears
we share. Thank you for my friends and the love and support
they never cease to give me. Thank you for my work, which
fulfills me and pays my bills. Thank you for this lovely home,
which reflects the joyful lives of those who dwell within.
These are my miracles, God, and I am so grateful
for each and every one.

HEARTS OVERFLOWING

Blessed are the pure in heart, for they will see God.
—Matthew 5:8

As the day gives way to night, my home becomes a place of quiet and calm. It is during this time that I remember each happy event of the day. As the light gives way to dark, my heart overflows with gratitude for all the love that fills these rooms, day in and day out. I pray that this will always be a home filled with happiness, but even when we as a family are faced with rough waters, I pray we will stick together and hold fast to our faith, knowing that God's loving care is the greatest blessing of all.

TOO MANY TO COUNT

*T*onight I started to count my blessings—until I realized I had far too many to count! My life is so filled with good things it would take a week's time to list them all. Suffice it to say that I am deeply grateful for all my blessings, even the ones that don't look like blessings at first. For it is in those challenges that I am given a real opportunity to know who I am and what I am capable of. I know I can always lean on you in hard times, Lord, but what a blessing it is to know I can first reach within myself for the courage and faith you've given me over the years.

Count your blessings, name them one by one:
Count your blessings, see what God hath done.
—Johnson Oatman, Jr.

Comfort and Hope

No More Tears

For thus says the Lord... As a mother comforts her
child, so will I comfort you.
—Isaiah 66:12–13

*T*onight I pray to be comforted like a child cradled
in the loving safety of its mother's arms. Rock me to sleep,
Lord, and take from my heart its heavy burdens so that I may
find the rest and emotional healing I seek. Bring me dreams
of fresh, new hopes for a brighter tomorrow filled with
miracles yet to unfold. I have wept many tears, but with you
to support me, I believe I am now ready to stand tall
and open wide the curtains of sadness to reveal the joyful
blessings waiting just beyond. Comfort me tonight, Lord,
and tomorrow will take care of itself.

LOST AND FOUND

*L*ord, help me to recover my lost self. I have been sad for so long that I cannot even begin to think about a good life. Help me find acceptance. As I go about my day tomorrow, help me cope with the spiral of sadness and despair. Give me the strength to get through each coming day a little more intact. Fill me with the hope of a new dawn that I may see the sunrise once again.

Though we may not think there is something to gain
in the depths of despair, it is only when we begin to heal
that we finally see the truth.

SEND ME AN ANGEL

Likewise the Spirit helps us in our weakness; for we do not know how to pray as we ought, but that very Spirit intercedes with sighs too deep for words.

—Romans 8:26

Lord, it's been a trying day, and I am bone-tired and weary. I pray for a renewed sense of hope to get me through the night and a renewed strength of spirit to face whatever tomorrow may bring. Send me an angel to watch over me as I sleep, and when the morning finally comes, I will be ready. With you by my side, offering your heavenly assistance, there is always a reason to hope for the best.

BLESSING FOR THIS NIGHT

The day has been long, Lord, but that's water under the bridge. Bless me now with stillness and sleep. As I slumber, I sigh and turn over, knowing that night will usher in the day with new joys and possibilities, gifts from your ever-wakeful spirit.

I know my character is what I am in the dark when no one is watching and no one can see. Therefore, bless me in my solitude, because temptation is the greatest here, and the possibility of a setback looms large.

Night and day may we give you praise and thanks, because you have shown us that all things belong to you, and all blessings are gifts from you.
—Clement of Alexandria

THE GIFT OF A GOOD DAY

*The earth has yielded its increase; God, our God,
has blessed us. May God continue to bless us;
let all the ends of the earth revere him.*

—Psalm 67:6–7

God, I thank you for the gift of a good day. As night
approaches, I am feeling much stronger and more
hopeful about so many things in my life. With your
loving arms to hold me up, I believe I can finally go where
before I've feared to tread. With your gentle, comforting
presence, I know I need not fear the challenges ahead;
instead I welcome them as new opportunities to grow,
to learn, and to become who I truly am.

REACHING OUT

Now may our Lord Jesus Christ himself and God our Father, who loved us and through grace gave us eternal comfort and hope, comfort your hearts and strengthen them in every good work and word.
—2 Thessalonians 2:16–17

Knowing he needs encouragement, I pray for my friend, Lord. Lifting my heart to you on his behalf, may I not fail to reach my hand to his—just as you are holding mine.

If I can throw a single ray of light across the darkened pathway
of another; if I can aid some soul to clearer
sight of life and duty, and thus bless my brother;
if I can wipe from any human cheek a tear, I shall
not have lived my life in vain while here.

AWAY FROM LONELINESS

Turn to me and be gracious to me,
for I am lonely and afflicted.
—Psalm 25:16

*I*f I am lonely tomorrow, I will let my need for others move me closer to a potential friend.

The greatest disease in the West today is not TB or leprosy; it is being unwanted, unloved, and uncared for. We can cure physical diseases with medicine, but the only cure for loneliness, despair, and hopelessness is love.
—Mother Teresa, *A Simple Path*

MY ROCK

Blessed be the Lord ... my rock and my fortress,
my stronghold and my deliverer, my shield
in whom I take refuge.

—Psalm 144:1–2

As I turn in for the night, God, I pray for the comfort of your heavenly promise of love everlasting. My soul is agitated with thoughts and worries about my day, but for tonight I pray to find the rest I need in your strength and the renewal I seek in your presence. You are my comfort in my time of need, the foundation I stand upon when all else around me crumbles, and my rock when I venture into turbulent waters.

Security Blanket

*He delivers and rescues, he works signs
and wonders in heaven and on earth...*
—Daniel 6:27

ou are my comfort and my strength, my security
blanket when I feel small and scared and need to be wrapped
in love. You are my lighthouse beacon guiding me safely
through rocky seas. Lord, I pray for a night of restful sleep,
tucked safely in the mighty arms of heavenly angels sent to
protect me. May you always walk with me across the dark
landscape of night to the safe shores of a bright new dawn;
may you always keep me warm with your heavenly light.

RIVER OF HOPE

*H*ope is like a river that begins in the heart, flowing outward to touch everyone and everything it comes in contact with. Tonight I rest in the knowledge that my hope and faith will lead me to happiness and fulfillment I never could have found on my own. Let my prayer be for a constant and renewed hope that never ceases to nourish my spirit and my heart. I pray I always have hope, for without it my life would be dry and without light. May I also be a river of goodwill for others whose spirits have dried up and are in need of a drink of hope.

Hope is the aspiration of the soul,
the persistance of the mind,
and the affirmation of the heart.

SWEET SUSTENANCE

*For there shall be a sowing of peace; the vine shall
yield its fruit, the ground shall give its produce,
and the skies shall give their dew.*

—Zechariah 8:12

What sweet comfort I find each night in your
love, God! What steadfast care! What nourishment for
my body, mind, and spirit! I pray tonight for a deeper
awareness of your presence and a greater understanding
of your will. When I think all is lost, you alone give rest
to my tired soul, and you alone provide the encouragement
and inspiration my mind and heart need. I pray for
the sweetest comfort of your infinite and eternal
sustenance, the food that feeds my soul.

Forgiveness of Self and Others

Making Mistakes

*T*each me the gift of forgiveness, Lord, that I may bear with those who have hurt me badly. Teach me to detach and let go and to turn these situations over to you, because I do not handle them well. Most of all, teach me how to forgive myself for the mistakes that I make. I should know better, but I am only human. When I am not living your will, I mess up. I know that you always forgive me my transgressions, but I ask for the courage and strength to learn that most important of lessons—how to forgive myself.

Because none of us will ever be able to live a perfect life, we need to be understanding and practice forgiveness in our daily lives.

REFUGE

*J*n many different relationships, dear God,
I have found the elements of what makes me feel at home:
conversations with close friends, the smiles of helpful
neighbors, the laughter of family celebrations, and
especially the peace of your presence.

Wherever you have sprinkled love, joy, peace, patience,
kindness, goodness, faithfulness, and gentleness, there I have
discovered a place for my soul to rest—a place to call home.

Enter and bless this family, Lord, so that within our circle
quarrels are resolved and relationships mature; failures are
forgiven and new directions are found.

HURTING, NOT HELPING

God, forgive me tonight for all the things I have said and done during the day that may have hurt or offended another. Sometimes I react hastily, and my tongue can be very sharp and inflict a lot of pain. I pray for your grace and ask you to work through me to make me into a person who thinks before speaking or acting. I ask for forgiveness for all the ways I may have hurt, instead of helped, the ones I came in contact with.

To err is human. To forgive, divine.
—Alexander Pope

WAITING FOR THE LIGHT

*But when I looked for good, evil came; and when
I waited for light, darkness came. My inward parts
are in turmoil, and are never still; days of affliction
come to meet me. I go about in sunless gloom.*
—Job 30:26–28

*L*ord, Job's words concerning his inner turmoil
are like those of my friend, who is besieged with trouble
on every side. She tries so hard to handle her problems with
integrity and grace, but the troubles just keep multiplying.
Her prayers seem to go unanswered. I've tried to be of help
and ease her pain, but only you can do that, Lord. Please
take away her relentless darkness and help her to find the
sunlight of your peace again. Amen.

The beauty of the dawn follows even the darkest night.

CLEANING THE SLATE

I pray tonight for the inner strength to be able to forgive my loved one for hurting me so much. I get lost in the pain, and when I do, I become resentful and angry. Those emotions don't do anyone any good—especially me. God, show me how to forgive my loved one and clean the slate between us. I feel too much emotion to be able to do something so noble and pure right now, but I know it is truly the first step toward healing and moving on to a better way of living.

When we learn to forgive the past, we sow the seeds
for a glorious future.

PROBLEMATIC LOVE

*Pay attention to what you hear; the measure
you give will be the measure you get,
and still more will be given you.*

—Mark 4:24

It's nighttime again, and another day's worth
of experiences have taught me again that love comes with
problems of its own. Lord, I ask that you forgive me if I have
not handled these problems in the best way.

I am doing the best I can with what I have. I ask for your
help in learning how to forgive the ones I love when they
don't meet my expectations. I pray one day you will show
me how to love without any conditions at all. But for now,
learning to forgive is the first step.

CALMING DOWN

*F*ather in heaven, sometimes I feel anger welling up inside me, and I need to turn to you for counsel. Please stay near to me and help me find ways to express my emotions without harming another's feelings. Help me to not get so upset that I cannot see past my own feelings. I need to understand myself, express myself, and accept myself—all within the bounds of your teachings.

Anger must be expressed, or it turns in on itself.
The secret is to express it in ways that are not
damaging but productive.

STRENGTH TO FORGIVE

Whenever you stand praying, forgive, if you have anything against anyone; so that your Father in heaven may also forgive you your trespasses.

—Mark 11:25

I pray tonight to first forgive, then to understand. So many times people do things that leave me wondering "Why?" I sometimes feel like the entire world is ganging up on me and turning against me. I certainly felt that way today. But when I am feeling victimized, I turn inward, and remind myself that others are simply behaving as they know how. I want to be strong enough, inside and out, to forgive them, Lord. And perhaps wise enough to one day understand them as well.

Moving On

*G*od, the suffering I've experienced from my relationship ending has caused such deep wounds, I sometimes wonder if I will ever heal. Please help me to find the courage within to forgive my ex, and myself, for the problems that led to our relationship ending. After all, I know I was part of the problem, and it is harder to forgive myself, knowing I could have done better but did not. Give me the ability to learn from my mistakes and forgive others for theirs. Help me move on toward the light of a happier tomorrow.

Only by moving through the pain do we get to embrace the gift of healing and call it our own.

HARD ON MYSELF

*Cast away from you all the transgressions
that you have committed against me, and get
yourselves a new heart and a new spirit!*
—Ezekiel 18:31

I know I can be hard on myself, and I tend to set
the bar of personal expectations much higher than I should.
When I fail to reach it, I beat myself up emotionally. Lord,
I pray tonight for the grace of your love, because it is your
grace that gives me the strength to face myself in the mirror,
instead of demanding more and accepting less. I pray that
I can look at myself with love, kindness, and forgiveness,
because I need to forgive myself for my failures if I am ever
to get to a place where I can enjoy my successes.

Understanding God's Will

THE BLAME GAME

**I sought the Lord, and he answered me,
and delivered me from all my fears.**

—Psalm 34:4

When life goes awry, Lord, I need someone to blame, so I sometimes point my finger at you. Heaven help me, but I want it both ways: you as the sender as well as the fixer of trouble. Help me know that you don't will trouble, for what good could you possibly gain? And when the good you want for me isn't possible, I know you are always with me.

TRUSTING GOD

***Do not let your hearts be troubled,
and do not let them be afraid.***

—John 14:27

*T*here are many events in our lives over which we have
no control. However, we do have a choice either to endure
trying times and press on or to give up. The secret of sur-
vival, whether or not we question God's presence or his ability to help us, is remembering that our hope is in the fairness,
goodness, and justice of God. When we put our trust in the
character of a God who cannot fail us, we will remain faithful. Our trust and faithfulness produce the endurance that
sees us through the "tough stuff" we all face in this life.

WHY ME?

I am sure you've heard it asked a million times, God: Why me? Why have I been given this problem to deal with? I am afraid, and my life seems to be on a one-way path to a dark place. Yet you have not given up on me. God, give me the strength to deal with what is on my plate and the wisdom to understand that, although I cannot see it, there is indeed an answer to that great question: *Why me?* I pray your will for me includes a great healing, but if it takes me in a different direction, I pray to accept your plan for me.

Some people blame their lack of faith on their different circumstances. Yet rough situations are often the catalyst for displays of great faith.

IN STILLNESS

For you, O Lord, are my hope,
my trust, O Lord, from my youth.
—Psalm 71:5

I know that faith is what keeps me moving forward. But sometimes, too, my trust allows a leisure like this. For you, God, are the one who upholds all things. Even as I sit here in stillness, your breath keeps me breathing, your mind keeps me thinking, your love keeps me yearning for home.

A life of faith . . . enables us to see God in everything
and it holds the mind in a state of readiness for
whatever may be his will.
—François Fenelon

MOVING FORWARD

The name of the Lord is a strong tower;
the righteous run into it and are safe.

—Proverbs 18:10

I am still moving, God, through storms. By your grace, over rough country you have carried me; amid pounding waves you have held me; beyond the horizon of my longings you have shown me your purposes. Even in this small room, sitting still, I am moving, God. Closer.

I'll admit it: Worry sometimes diminishes my faith. I get anxious about my family's safety and health, about job security and bills—even about vacations and the weather! But I know, Lord, that when I get anxious, all I need to do is take a deep breath and remember that it's all in your hands, not mine.

THIS WAY OR THAT

Happy is the one who listens to me, watching
daily at my gates, waiting beside my doors.
—Proverbs 8:34

God, I am at a crossroads in my life, and I don't know
which way to go. Both paths have their good and
bad points, and my will and mind don't seem to be
helping me in making a decision. I pray for a sign of
your will for me, that you may lovingly guide me to the
one path that is truly for my highest good and the good
of those concerned. I pray I will recognize this sign and that
I will have the faith and courage to follow your lead.
Only you know the right way.

WHY AM I HERE?

I pray tonight for clarity of my purpose here on earth.
Lately I've been feeling as though my life has no real
meaning or depth. I do the best I can, but I want a deeper
calling, something that will lend my days purpose. Lord,
I pray for a clear vision of what your intended path is for me
in this lifetime. I want to put my talents and skills to
the highest and best use and to give the love I know I was
put here to give. Show me the way.

Remember you are the promise and the hope of the future.
Remember you are the very essence of life.
Remember you are born for a purpose.

Not Ours to Know

Happy are those who keep my ways.
Hear instruction and be wise, and do not neglect it.
—Proverbs 8:32–33

*L*ord, I know your ways are not always ours to know
or understand, but I am suffering the loss of a loved one,
and I long to know that this, too, is part of your will for
all of our lives. The pain is often hard to bear, but knowing
that this is all a part of a greater destiny takes away some
of the grief. I pray to understand even just one small part
of the puzzle that is the mystery of life, Lord. Your ways are
not always ours, but I have faith in your ways nonetheless.

Broke or Blessed?

For my thoughts are not your thoughts,
nor are your ways my ways, says the Lord.
For as the heavens are higher than the earth,
so are my ways higher than your ways...
—Isaiah 55:8–9

I recently lost my job, Lord, and I'm really worried. I have a family to support, bills to pay, and a house to take care of. I am angry and hurt and afraid, but I have faith in your will for my life, and I hold fast to the understanding that once this is all over, I will find a new door opened before me filled with incredible new opportunities. I may be lost, broken, and even broke, but I pray that with your love to guide me, I will open the door to rich, new blessings and an even better job.

Through the Fog

**No lion shall be there, nor shall any ravenous
beast come up on it; they shall not be found there,
but the redeemed shall walk there.**

—Isaiah 35:9

*M*y prayer tonight is for clarity. I have some
persistent problems, and lately it feels like I'm walking
through a thick haze or fog, with no direction and nothing
to guide me. I pray for a clear path and a clear vision about
how to walk that path. I want to reach the other side! Your
will is not obvious to me, God, but I trust in it and will keep
on walking until I see that opening in the fog, which offers
wonderful glimpses of clear skies ahead.

MIXED SIGNALS

One does not live by bread alone, but by every word that comes from the mouth of God.
—Matthew 4:4

Wow, a potential new love in my life! The only thing is, I am getting mixed inner signals as to whether this is a person I should trust or not. I've been hurt deeply before, and I feel I can no longer rely on my own emotional radar.

Help me to know the right thing to do. If this relationship is your will, God, then I will learn to trust, and try to open myself to love again. I pray tonight for your will to be known. My faith in you is strong, and I know you only want the best for me.

Surrender: Turning It Over to God

PRESENT BLESSINGS

*D*ear God, help me to focus my thoughts more upon what I have than what I lack. May my heart lay hold of present realities rather than future possibilities.

For I know this moment—the now—is all we are given. Whether we are sick or healthy, this juncture in time is the place we share. Bless us in this moment, needing nothing to change. Let us simply be in your presence,
just for this moment.

Lord, in the midst of life's troubles, you come to us. In the darkness, your Spirit moves, spreading light like a shower of stars against a stormy night sky.

NOTHING BUT GOD

Let us therefore desire nothing else, wish for nothing else, and let nothing please and delight us except our Creator and Redeemer, and Savior, the only true God, who is full of good, who alone is good, ... and from whom, and through whom, and in whom is all mercy, all grace, all glory of all penitents and of the just, and of all the blessed rejoicing in heaven.

—St. Francis of Assisi

For St. Francis, it's not all *or* nothing.
It's all *and* nothing.

Even if we receive and delight only in God's gifts, we end up with all the mercy, grace, glory, and joy that heaven has to offer. When we surrender ourselves entirely to the Lord, we will get everything that truly matters. In essence, we give up things that don't last, and we receive things that do.

It's not a bad trade.

Moving Beyond Fear

Strengthen the weak hands, and make firm the feeble knees. Say to those who are of a fearful heart, "Be strong, do not fear!"

—Isaiah 35:3–4

I am sitting here tonight, anxious for what tomorrow might bring. I start a new life tomorrow, and all those old anxieties are popping up again. God, I know the only way to move beyond fear is to go through it, so I am turning it all over to you, trusting that whatever is meant to happen will happen, and that I will have the strength to deal with anything that comes my way. I will keep my focus on the good in my life, and on your steadfast belief in me, even when I doubt myself.

TAKE IT ALL, GOD

***Cast your burden on the Lord, and he will sustain
you, he will never permit the righteous to be moved.***
—Psalm 55:22

God, I don't want these burdens anymore. It seems
like they're just too much to carry alone. Take
them, take it all, and do your will with my life. I put my
faith and trust in you and in the outcome you have chosen
for me. I am letting go of my need to try and fix things
I simply have no control over. I pray tonight, as I go to bed,
that tomorrow will bring the peace of surrender and
release from the anxieties I've been facing. I know my faith
in you will help see me through. Amen.

HEAVINESS

Take care that you do not forget the Lord.
—Deuteronomy 6:12

*M*y heart is heavy, God. I realize now at the
end of the day that I haven't thought of you once. I haven't
considered how you would want me to act, whether you had
something for me to do, or if anything I did was
simply against your Word.

It's so silly. I know I can't do this on my own, yet today
I took on the whole world as though I'm the only person
who counts. Please forgive me.

Help me not to slide so far into my own plans that
I forget your timetable is far more important than anything
I could come up with. Again, forgive me, and let me be
always mindful of your presence in my life.

TAKING CONTROL

**Blessed rather are those who hear the word
of God and obey it!**
—Luke 11:28

*T*onight I pray for the gift of surrender. I cannot seem
to make things change in my life right now, and I know I am
trying to control people and situations, forcing my will. God,
I now surrender it all to you, because only your will can truly
make things happen in my life. When I try to take the reins,
remind me that you alone know my life's higher calling.
When I try to force the issue, gently guide me to turn it all
over to you. Thank you, God, for taking control.

CARRY ME

**For God alone my soul waits in silence,
from him comes my salvation.**

**He alone is my rock and my salvation, my fortress;
I shall never be shaken.**

—Psalm 62:1–2

*L*ord, tonight I want to thank you for giving me
clear signs, reminding me that I need to let go and let you
take control. When I give up my struggle and allow you to
carry me through the places I cannot walk alone, things
always turn out better. It's something I need to work on
and be reminded of often, but this letting go stuff really
works! With you to take on my struggles, I know I have
a life partner I can always count on in times of need.
Your grace is amazing.

RELEASE

But for you who revere my name the sun of
righteousness shall rise, with healing in its wings.
You shall go out leaping like calves from the stall.
—Malachi 4:2

God, I've been in pain for so long, I don't know how much more this poor body can take. I need the release that comes from complete surrender, and I am turning my pain over to you for healing. I cannot do it alone. But with you, God, all things are possible; with your love I know I can get through another night and that the morning will bring some relief. But I know that first I have to turn my pain over to you. I pray I find the courage to keep releasing my doubt and my fear. May I find healing now.

ONE DAY AT A TIME

I pray tonight for the courage to turn over this awful addiction to you, my Higher Power. The only way I can stay sober is to surrender my will to you, God, for you alone can heal me. I pray for the serenity that comes from accepting that I am an addict, for that is the first step toward complete sobriety. With you at my side, I can learn to live life one day at a time and continue to surrender my will when I feel that craving to use a substance again. One day at a time, God. I can do this.

God grant me the serenity to accept the things I cannot change, courage to change the things I can, and wisdom to know the difference.
—Reinhold Niebuhr

WITH THE FLOW

God, I've worked so hard all my life, but I still can't seem to be able to feel happy and secure at the end of the day. I want my dreams to come true, but sometimes it feels like I am swimming against the tide. My way isn't working, and so I surrender my will and my life to you. Your wisdom is much greater than mine, and the dreams you have for me are much grander than anything I could envision. From this night on, I pray to always go with the flow and live your will, God, instead of fighting the tide. Amen.

It is not the going out of port, but the coming in, that determines the success of a voyage.
—Henry Ward Beecher

Peace and Serenity

A NEW DAY IS DAWNING

*W*e toss and turn, God of nighttime peace, making lists of "must do" and "should have done." We wind up feeling unequal to the tasks and sleep-deprived to boot. Bless us with deep sleep and dreams that reveal us as you see us: beloved, worthy, capable. At dawn, help us see possibilities on our lists.

Each time we yawn today, Lord—for it was a short night—we'll breathe in your restorative presence and exhale worries. Tonight we'll sleep like the sheep of your pasture, for we lie down and rise up in your care, restored, renewed, and rested.

Have courage for the great sorrows of life and patience for the small ones; and when you have laboriously accomplished your daily task, go to sleep in peace. God is awake.

—Victor Hugo

A PEACEFUL HOME

Whatever house you enter, first say,
"Peace to this house!"
—Luke 10:5

There's been a lot of chaos around this house lately. The fighting must end, for it is hurting everyone. Tonight I pray for peace for all those who dwell in this house, that each of us first may find peace within and then peace among each other. I ask for your gift of eternal and everlasting peace for everyone in this house. May your peace cover us like a loving blanket as we sleep, and may we all awaken to a morning filled with calmness and serenity.

TRULY SERENE

I will both lie down and sleep in peace;
for you alone, O Lord, make me lie down in safety.
—Psalm 4:8

God, I know I cannot ever be at peace with someone
else in my life until I first learn to be at peace
with myself. I pray tonight for that calm that surpasses
all understanding, a serenity that fills the heart and calms
the spirit. I want to move on from this stressful, unhappy
situation, and I realize I can only do that if I can find a steady
place inside myself from which to deal with others. There
has been so much turmoil, and I pray for calm
waters on which to float.

BLESS THIS FAMILY

*B*less these children, God.
Keep them growing in mind and body. Keep them ever
moving and reaching out toward the objects of their
curiosity. And may they find, in all their explorations,
the one thing that holds it all together: your love.

Thank you for the gift of ancestral faith. As I take my place in
the family portrait, may I continue to keep you, everlasting
God, as the centerpiece of our family, for your love is as ageless
and steadfast as the wind calling my name. Watch over the
grandchildren as you have over me in your special ways. Listen
as I call out their names in echoes of those family prayers
shared on my behalf through a lifetime of faithful love.

IT IS WHAT IT IS

*L*ord, I've been fighting this situation over and over, unable to accept it and move on. I know it is making me crazy and sick inside, and I pray tonight for your peace, the peace that only you can give me. I am tired of struggling, and I want to wake up renewed. I want to remain calm and know that I am able to accept what comes my way with a clear head. I don't like fighting and conflict, and I don't want to invite any more of it into my life. Show me instead, God, the ways of peace. So let it be.

Growing in wisdom means growing in love, tolerance, grace, and acceptance.

THE CALM SURFACE

**Put out into the deep water
and let down your nets for a catch.**
—Luke 5:4

I know, God, that often we are deceived by a calm surface, and that below the surface there is great disorder. I feel that way now, like a pond that looks serene yet is filled with bustling fish below. I pray this night to be filled with a deeper serenity, one that reaches from the surface to the very bottom of my soul. I pray this night to be still, knowing the presence of your loving power within me. That power gives me peace, and I need that peace tonight.

FINALLY OVER

*And the peace of God, which surpasses all
understanding, will guard your hearts and your
minds in Christ Jesus.*

—Philippians 4:7

Thank you, Lord, for being by my side during
such a difficult time. For the first night in a long time,
I feel completely at peace. My hope for a better life has
been renewed, and my spirit feels light tonight, ready
for a good rest. There will be much to do in the morning,
but for tonight I am calm in the knowledge that you
have helped me through a very dark time.
Because of your love, I am at peace.

ENOUGH ALREADY!

My relationship has been filled lately with
nothing but anger and hostility. Enough already! I pray
tonight for a peace to settle upon me and my loved one,
a peace that fills both our spirits with a sense of
tranquility and calm. We love each other, but without
peace our relationship will never survive. I pray we both
find serenity within ourselves as well as with one another.
Show us the way to heal our relationship and
take us back to love again.

Whatever the relationship, forgiveness is a truly healing gift for
the people involved.

Nothing New

**What has been is what will be,
and what has been done is what will be done;
there is nothing new under the sun.**

—Ecclesiastes 1:9

What a fast-paced, constantly changing world
we live in! Does anything ever stay the same?

Yes! When it comes to the inner life—the essential needs
and longings, the motives and goals of us all—these things
have always been the same and will remain so.

For just a moment, I'll recall that the undercurrents
of my spiritual life flow deeper than this stormy,
wave-tossed surface.

PRECIOUS SOLITUDE

God, there is nothing like a walk before bedtime to
make me realize how precious living alone can
be. In the quiet of the coming night, I feel at peace
with myself and with the world. Nature is all around me,
and my loved ones are healthy and happy. I am at peace
with my dreams, ambitions, and goals, and everything in
this moment is simply and utterly serene. I know it won't
last and that the morning may bring loud noise and chaos,
but for now I bask in the precious solitude of just
being at peace with you.

In the solitude of a natural setting, the heart discovers serenity,
the soul knows abiding peace, and the spirit
finds renewal.

LET IT BEGIN WITH ME

Then justice will dwell in the wilderness, and righteousness abide in the fruitful field.
—Isaiah 32:16

I love the idea of being a catalyst for calmness. Tonight, I pray that you will work through me to spread peace in the world, starting right here in my own home. Let me be a vessel filled with words and actions that make others feel happy and calm. Help me drop the sharp tongue and hotheadedness. I know that true peace in the world, if we are ever to achieve such a dream, must begin at home. Let it begin with me, God; let me be a picture of the calm I want to see in the world.

Ending the Day

INTO THE NIGHT

You saw how the Lord your God carried you,
just as one carries a child, all the way that you
traveled until you reached this place.

—Deuteronomy 1:31

*T*hank you, Lord, for being my companion throughout the day. Though many things are pulling me in many directions, I know you will keep me on course to do what is truly important. Thank you as well for listening to me and counseling me when I needed to verbally unwind or when I needed advice. As I end the day, I am thankful for your presence. This I pray. Amen.

PROTECTOR OF MY SOUL

God, another long day has passed, and I am ready to turn in for the night. I pray you will protect my loved ones and me as darkness sets in, and that my soul shall find safe harbor in your grace. May I find the rest my body longs for and my spirit needs, and may I awaken to a bright new day in the comfort of your love.

Under his wings I am safely abiding,
though the night deepens and tempests are wild;
still I can trust him, I know he
will keep me,
he has redeemed me and I am his child.
—William O. Cushing

OVERNIGHT FAITH

Weeping may linger for the night,
but joy comes with the morning.
—Psalm 30:5

od, give me "overnight faith," the kind of faith that
gets me through the darkness with my eyes clearly
focused on the light of a new dawn rising. Help me sleep
peacefully in the security of your care and comfort,
even though right now I feel anything but calm in my mind.
Let me leave my cares with you and instead wrap myself
in the blanket of your loving grace. I look to you and lean
on you in hard times, for your strength never wavers.
I know I am never alone.

THE PERFECT END

What a wonderful gift this entire day has been! I now prepare for the night with a heart full of joy and gratitude for blessings received and with a spirit of expectancy and hope for more blessings to come. This day has been perfect, and my deep faith allows me to rest assured, knowing the night will be peaceful and restful as well. Thank you for a glorious end to a glorious day!

Through love to light!
Oh wonderful the way,
That leads from darkness
to the perfect day!
—Richard Watson Gilder, "After Song"

WRAPPING UP

Almighty God, I haven't failed to notice that each day begins with a sunrise and ends with a sunset. I know that's your way of wrapping us in your glory. That you created me—you who also placed the stars in the sky and caused the tides to ebb and flow—sometimes is more than I can comprehend. You alone are the source of every breath I take. Great and mighty are you, God, and in this I offer my praise.

Lord, may I be wakeful at sunrise to begin a new day for you, cheerful at sunset for having done my work for you; thankful at moonrise and under starshine for the beauty of the universe. And may I add what little may be in me to your great world.
—The Abbot of Greve

LAYING THE DAY TO REST

**_It was no messenger or angel but his
presence that saved them; in his love and
in his pity he redeemed them._**

—Isaiah 63:9

This has been a trying day, filled with challenges
and difficulties, and I pray the coming night is filled with
peace. Now it is time to lay the day to rest and give my spirit
some respite as well. God, I pray your presence will get me
through the night, knowing your love will redeem me in the
morning. I go to bed tired and weary but know that your
strength will be there for me to draw upon as I sleep.

GOODNIGHT, GOD

*I*t's time to turn in, and I do so with a heart full of gratitude for all you have done for me today. There have been good moments and not-so-good moments throughout this day, and yet with you by my side, I've been able to experience both with an abundance of grace and humility. I pray the night will bring me deep, restful sleep and a renewed spirit in the morning, so I'm ready to do it all over again. Goodnight, God.

Blessings on him who invented sleep, the cloak that covers all human thoughts, the food that satisfies hunger, the drink that quenches thirst...
—Miguel de Cervantes

HOPEFUL NIGHT

*L*ord, while we are in the midst of mourning life's
troubles, you come to us. In the darkness, your spirit moves,
spreading light like a shower of stars against
a stormy night sky.

Teach us to know that it is exactly at the point of our deepest
despair that you are closest. For at those times we can finally
admit that we have wandered in the dark without a clue. Yet
you have been there with us all along. Thank you for your
abiding presence.

Hope, like the glimmering taper's light,
Adorns and cheers our way;
And still, as darker grows the night,
Emits a brighter ray.
—Oliver Goldsmith

THE ONE I CAN ALWAYS COUNT ON

I am the living bread that came down from heaven.
Whoever eats of this bread will live forever...

—John 6:51

As I prepare my family for the coming night,
I pray you will continue to love and guide me in all my ways.
I know that I can always count on you when I need you.
When I feel alone, you remind me I am never alone.
When I feel small, you show me my grandness. When I am
afraid, you infuse me with courage and faith to face
whatever stands before me. Thank you, God, for always
being there for me and for my family.

REST IN YOUR LIGHT

While you have the light, believe in the light,
so that you may become children of light.

—John 12:36

*H*eavenly Father, I pray that your light shines down upon me as I set about preparing for the night. May I always bask in the glow of your eternal and unceasing love, and may your wisdom inspire and guide me, even as I sleep. As the night sets in, I look to you for the beacon of faith that always permeates the darkness, and for the love that brings true rest to the body and spirit. I am but a lamp, asking to be lit by the one true light that shines above all else.

SOUND SLEEPERS

*ecurity, loving God, is going to sleep in
the assurance that you know our hearts before we speak,
and are waiting, as soon as you hear from us, to transform
our concerns into hope and action, our loneliness into
companionship, and our despair into dance.*

Source of all life and love, let this family be a place
of warmth on a cold night, a friendly haven for the
lonely stranger, a small sanctuary of peace in the midst
of swirling activity. Above all, let its members seek to reflect
the kindness of your own heart, day by day.